Lawrence of Arabia

Copyright © 1979, Macdonald-Raintree, Inc.

All rights reserved. No part of this book may be reproduced or utilized in any form or by any means, electronic or mechanical, including photocopying, recording, or by any information storage and retrieval system, without permission in writing from the Publisher. Inquiries should be addressed to Macdonald-Raintree, Inc., 205 West Highland Avenue, Milwaukee, Wisconsin 53203.

Library of Congress Number: 78-31450

1 2 3 4 5 6 7 8 9 0 83 82 81 80 79

Printed and bound in the United States of America.

Library of Congress Cataloging in Publication Data

Ebert, Richard.
    Lawrence of Arabia.

    SUMMARY: Recounts the adventures of the British soldier who helped the Arabs gain freedom from the Turks during World War I.
    1. Lawrence, Thomas Edward, 1888-1935 — Juvenile literature. 2. Soldiers — England — Biography — Juvenile literature. 3. European War, 1914-1918 — Campaigns — Turkey and the Near East — Juvenile literature. [1. Lawrence, Thomas Edward, 1888-1935. 2. Soldiers. 3. World War, 1914-1918 — Campaigns — Turkey and the Near East] I. Schofield, Roy Malcolm. II. Title.
D568.4.L45E23   940.4'15'0924 [B] [92]   78-31450
ISBN 0-8393-0150-2 lib. bdg.

Lawrence of Arabia

By
Richard Ebert

Illustrations by
Roy Schofield

Raintree Publishers
Milwaukee • Toronto • Melbourne • London

One of the most famous men of World War I was Thomas Edward Lawrence. When the war began in 1914, only a few people knew him. When the war ended in 1918, the whole world knew him as . . . Lawrence of Arabia.

As a young boy he had many hobbies. He was very interested in the past and spent many happy hours cycling around the countryside visiting old churches. He learned to make brass rubbings of carvings on tombs.

As Lawrence grew older his main interest was in archaeology — studying how people in the past lived. At first he worked in Britain, but soon he went to other countries. In 1909 he traveled to Syria, Palestine, and Arabia. He learned to love the Arab lands and got along very well with the Arab people. He soon learned to speak their language and to live as they did.

For hundreds of years the Arab lands had been ruled by the Turks. Many Arabs hoped that one day they would rule their own country again. However, there was so much jealousy between the Arab tribes that this didn't seem possible.

In 1914 Lawrence joined a group of surveyors that set out to map parts of Arabia. A few months later, just after Lawrence had returned to England, World War I broke out. The war was fought mostly in Europe. However, the Middle East — where the Arab lands are — was important too. The Turks were fighting on the side of Britain's enemies, so the Arabs became important to the British.

7

Lawrence's knowledge of the Arabs and their lands was now very useful. He became an officer in the army and went to Cairo.

In Cairo he learned that the Arabs were planning to rise against the Turks. Arabia's leader, King Hussein, began the revolt. Lawrence went to talk with him.

Lawrence quickly won the trust of the Arab leaders. He got along well with the Emir Feisal, one of King Hussein's sons. By the end of the year, Lawrence was working at Feisal's headquarters. Lawrence began to wear Arab clothes after Feisal suggested it to him.

King Hussein and the Arabs drove the Turks from a large stretch of the coast. Next the Arabs tried to attack the important city of Medina, but they didn't have a chance. They were mounted on horses and camels and did not have enough rifles and ammunition. The Turkish machine guns and artillery were too much for the Arabs. The attack was a failure.

Lawrence knew that the Arabs were eager to defeat the Turks. But at that time the Arabs were practically helpless. Lawrence told Feisal that Britain would send guns, ammunition, and gold. When five British warships arrived, things began to look better for the Arabs.

Feisal made his headquarters in a town on the coast. When he learned that a large force of Turks was planning a night attack, the British warships were made ready. The night of the attack was very dark and still. Suddenly the warships' searchlights pierced the darkness, lighting up the Turkish soldiers. They stopped, turned, and began to run.

Instead of fighting large battles, Lawrence began a campaign of guerrilla attacks against the Turks. Lawrence, with just a few men, would strike suddenly at points that were important to the Turks. Attacks on bridges and railway lines kept supplies from reaching the Turks. Fighting in this way, the Arabs on camels were successful against the machine guns of a modern army.

A band of Arabs, with Lawrence as the leader, would lie in wait behind the sand dunes near a railway. After putting explosives on the tracks, they would wait for the train. When it was close enough, they set off the explosives. The engine and a part of the track would shoot upwards in a cloud of sand, dust, and pieces of flying metal. Then Lawrence and his men would dash out to attack the Turkish guards.

Lawrence described one of these attacks in a letter to a friend, "The last stunt was the hold-up of a train. It has two locomotives, and we gutted one with an electric mine."

Lawrence went on to describe how the Arabs and the Turks shot back and forth at each other for a few minutes. "Then we tried a Stokes gun, and two beautiful shots dropped right in the middle of them. They could not stand that and bolted away . . . The whole job took ten minutes."

After an attack the Arabs swarmed over the train taking any supplies they could find. They forced open the freight cars and rushed back and forth with their loot. The Turks were very anxious to capture the leader of these attacks. They knew him as El Aurens, the name that the Arabs had given to Lawrence.

By working together, Lawrence and Feisal had done what others thought impossible. Their victories made Arab tribes that had once been rivals ready to come together to fight under one flag. They all wanted to free the Arab lands from the Turks and rule their country themselves.

The conditions in the desert were hard, even for people who had lived there all their lives. Lawrence proved that he was as tough and skillful as the Arab warriors. He could run alongside a camel, swing up into the saddle, and ride as fast as anyone else.

Lawrence and a group of tough desert fighters planned to attack the important town of Akaba. But first they had to travel across many miles of harsh desert. Just before they reached Akaba, they were stopped at a Turkish stronghold in the mountains. For a time it looked as though they might not be able to get past it.

Then one of the Arab leaders, Auda, called on his men to mount their horses and follow him. A few minutes later they charged wildly at the Turkish guns. Next Lawrence, with 400 soldiers on camels screaming behind him, attacked the position too. The Turks broke and ran, with the Arabs following close behind. By nightfall the battle was over. News of the victory spread to other Arab tribes.

The rest of the army moved on to Akaba, which soon surrendered to the Arabs.

The British were very pleased when they heard that Akaba had been captured by the Arabs. They promised to send guns and ammunition, armored cars, aircraft, and British officers to aid the Arab guerrillas.

Lawrence continued leading raids against the Turkish railway. After one raid Lawrence found himself alone. The others had disappeared with the loot.

Some attacks did not go well. Once Lawrence was hit by a piece of flying metal when a train was blown up. He fell down between the firing from both sides. Some of his men were killed trying to rescue him, but others dragged him to safety. The train was too heavily defended, and the Arabs had to retreat. They carried the wounded Lawrence with them.

Sometimes Lawrence went to spy on the Turks. Once he was caught by the Turks, imprisoned and whipped. After he was released, he struggled back to his men in the desert.

The Arabs captured Tafileh, a town on the Red Sea. Soon after they had taken it, the Turks attacked in great force. Many of the Arabs fled as the Turks began firing with machine guns. Shells and shrapnel burst on the town. Lawrence and the Arabs held on grimly. They were waiting for help to arrive from nearby tribes.

During a lull in the fighting, the Arabs crept quietly from rock to rock. Soon they were near the Turkish machine-gun posts. At the same time another group of Arabs on horses attacked from the side. The Turks began to retreat. Lawrence and his men captured every Turkish gun, horse, and mule. Only a few of the Turks who had attacked Tafileh returned alive. It was a great victory for Lawrence and the Arabs.

Soon after this, the Turkish army began to retreat from the Arab lands. However, Lawrence and his guerrillas kept up their attacks for several months until the war was over, late in 1918. Eventually, Lawrence returned to England.

Many years later, in 1935, Lawrence was killed in a motor bike accident in England. But he is still remembered as Lawrence of Arabia, the great hero who fought in the desert.